Twelve Things You Need To Know Before You Graduate

About the Author:

After four years of undergraduate work at Auburn University and three years of graduate work at the University of Alabama, Anne L. Willingham left school with a shiny new Master of Fine Arts Diploma and went out into the world to seek her fortune. Luckily enough, her parents agreed to feed her while she was looking for work. Through hard work/Providence/sheer luck, she managed to find a way to pay her bills. Her parents are very grateful and, quite frankly, never thought she'd do it with a theatre degree.

Over the years Anne has built sets, painted sets, designed both sets and lights, pushed roadcases, hung lights, fought with fog machines and set off numerous smoke alarms, taught college, stage managed, worked with actors/dancers/directors, lifeguarded, coached swimming, carved Styrofoam, sold lighting equipment, worked with high school teachers and done pretty much whatever would bring in some income. This should be your first lesson about graduation. You are only beginning to learn.

Table of Contents:

Section One- The Person You Are
- Chapter 1- Character
- Chapter 2- Work Ethic
- Chapter 3- Time Management
- Chapter 4- Punctuality

Section Two: Finding a Job
- Chapter 5- Marketing Yourself
- Chapter 6- Networking
- Chapter 7- Interview Skills
- Chapter 8- Types of Jobs
- Chapter 9- Traditional vs. Non-traditional Jobs

Section Three: Money, Money, Money
- Chapter 10- Budgeting
- Chapter 11- Taxes

Section Four: The World of Theatre
- Chapter 12- Unions and LORT

BONUS Chapter 13- Discretion

Introduction

So you have managed to slog through four plus years of higher education and you are screaming up on graduation. Now what do you do? Your parents, of course, pretty desperately want you to get a job. You're cute and all, but dreadfully expensive. They are ready for you to be settled and off their payroll. You are also probably ready to be an independent adult, with the income to match it. Sadly, you have picked a major with limited income potential, so you are going to have to be clever about it. There are also eleventy billion other theatre majors getting ready to flood the marketplace so your odds are even worse. It's enough to make you seriously consider just staying in school forever, right?

No, no, it's okay. Buck up, little cowboy. You CAN, in fact, make a decent living in theatre. You won't be loaded and will pretty much have to kiss away the thought of owning that Porsche, but let's face it, you are much better served with a beat up old pickup truck anyway. You are going into theatre. You will at some point need to haul things.

This book has twelve chapters (plus a bonus one for the ladies). All are based on real conversations with real theatre people. Your illustrious author went around to real actors and real techs and asked them what they wished someone had told them when they were fresh out of school. These twelve plus chapters cover those topics. Well, and some things my dad told me that I really, really wish I had listened to when I was in my 20s. Turns out, he was right.

This book, while mainly geared towards technical theatre graduates, is equally useful for actors as well. The same truths hold. Pay attention and be one of the good actors.

Section One- The Person You Are

"Optimist: someone who isn't sure whether life is a tragedy or a comedy but is tickled silly just to be in the play." Robert Brault[1]

Chapter One: Character

Your character matters. It is true. The world of theatre is a fairly tiny world. For most of us it is more like four degrees of separation instead of six. No matter what city you end up in everybody will know somebody that knows you. That can be the best thing ever or the worst. So who you are matters. People will hear about your character, so it is in your best interest to have a good one. This chapter looks at four aspects of your character that employers care about. Quite frankly, most people I know that are hiring would prefer that you have these qualities rather than be the smartest kid in the program. They can usually

[1] http://izquotes.com/quote/291769

teach you the skills. It is really hard to teach you character.

Attitude

Merriam Webster defines attitude as "a feeling or way of thinking that affects a person's behavior".[2] Basically, your attitude is either good or bad. Positive or negative. And it is your choice which way it goes. It is all up to you.

A positive attitude will get you far. Trust me on this one. I'm not saying that you need to be "Miss Mary Sunshine" or, heaven forbid, perky. Perky is just generally annoying and someone will eventually have to staple you to the floor or gaff tape your mouth closed to keep the rainbows and sunshine from spewing out. But you need to be the person seeing the glass as half full. Why? A positive attitude will drive you forward and get you jobs. A negative attitude is contagious, affects the working environment and is physically

---

[2] http://www.merriam-webster.com/dictionary/attitude

stressful. If you are Mr./Ms. Negativity, then odds are you are only going to be offered work as a last option. I know that when we make decisions about who to put on a call, personality comes into play. If you are negative and a thorn in the crew chief/director/stage manager's side, you probably aren't going to get another gig with us. Play nice. Be sweet. Your mother was right when she told you that.

Ways to Avoid a Negative Attitude

<u>Realize that the world does not owe you anything</u>. I realize that you probably have received a trophy for every extracurricular event you have ever participated in ever, but the truth is that you are only special to a very few people. You are not special to most of the planet. You are just some guy/girl that needs a job. And since there are half a dozen other people vying for the same job, you are not special. Do you have any idea how many theatre majors graduate each and every year?

Be flexible. Change happens. Change happens a LOT in our industry. Directors change their minds. Designers change their minds. Actors spontaneously change their blocking. Clients change their minds. Go into a project knowing that lots of things, perhaps everything, will change at least once. Deal with it and move on. If you get whiny, no one will want to play with you.

Part B of being flexible is about job choices. Hopefully you have learned all sorts of things while in school and are multi-talented. You might want a job as a stage manager, but there might not be any stage management jobs available. Be flexible enough to take the lighting job or the props job or whatever work is available. The more jobs you can do, the more likely your odds of staying employed all the time. I started out as a set designer. When I got out of grad school there were no scenic jobs available. There were lighting gigs available though. Now I am known as a lighting designer. Life changes. Roll with it. In my past I have been a stage hand, stage manager, lighting tech, lighting designer, scenic artist, scenic charge artist, scenic designer, teacher, salesman, and lifeguard. Don't limit your skill set to just theatre.

<u>Choose to see the good in situations.</u> There is almost always something good in every situation. I hate to sound like Mary Poppins here, but really there is. It might only be that you have a job with a paycheck that means you can pay your rent and maybe get a frappuchino to go. But, hey, that is a good thing. Your life will be more fun if you can manage to see the humor in situations. Life for the most part is fairly entertaining. Look for it. Be the fun person on the call or in the cast. We are theatre people. If it isn't fun at some level you really should have picked a different major.

<u>Use what you have been given</u>. We are all dealt out skills and abilities. While we can develop those innate talents, there will always be someone else with more or different talents. Deal with it. We cannot all look like movie

stars. We cannot all have mad design skills. We cannot all have everything. Figure out what you are good at and do that. Everyone has something that they are really, really good at. It might be weird. It might be quirky. It might be random. But you are good at something. Know what it is and work on it. Then put it on your resume.

<u>Know that life isn't always fair.</u> I grew up hearing my dad say this. He said it a LOT. Actually what he said was "Life's not fair, pal." And it is true. Life is absolutely not fair. There is nothing you can do to make it fair. Griping about the unfairness of it all will not change a darn thing. Get over it and deal with what you do have. There will always be someone that gets a job you want. There will possibly be a job that by rights should be yours that goes to someone else that is much less qualified. In a perfect world everything would work out, well... perfectly. But life is not fair and is never going to be. Deal with it and move on, people. It is what it is. You might also keep in mind that everyone else is dealing

with the unfairness of life, even if you can't see how their world is unfair. We are all in this together, so be gentle and play nice. You never know what the other guy is dealing with.

Your attitude is your choice. You make the decision every morning when you roll out of bed. Will I be positive today or will I be in a mood? Know that people remember your attitude. Those that are pleasant to be around and fun to work with ultimately get more work. Be that person.

Chapter Two: Work Ethic

"Many of the great achievements of the world were accomplished by tired and discouraged men who kept on working." Anonymous[3]

Mirriam Webster defines work ethic as "a belief in work as a moral good." [4] The common definition of someone with a GOOD work ethic is someone that will work hard and be dependable. Is that you?

With apologies to the Boy Scouts (and to my father who quoted this to me a bunch when I was a kid), I present traits of a good work ethic.

<u>Be trustworthy</u>. This means being honest and truthful all the time. Dishonesty and lies will catch up with you. Theatre people gossip and

---

[3] http://thinkexist.com/quotations/perseverance/

[4] http://www.merriam-webster.com/dictionary/work%20ethic

absolutely cannot keep secrets. If you lie to a boss/director they will find out eventually. No more work for you! Learn to keep your mouth shut.

Be loyal. Most of you will start out by freelancing. You will work for multiple companies at the same time. Loyalty means supporting those that are supporting you. Do not badmouth company A to company B. Do not talk bad about a director. They are giving you work. Disloyal employees do not last long and their reputation will preceed them. We all talk about each other in this industry.

Be helpful. Be the person that hops up to take care of things. Be the person that does a job that needs doing even when it isn't your responsibility. Be the person that picks trash up off the floor and throws it away. Be the person that helps carry things when the propsmaster/stage manager/crew chief has full hands. Be a helper. People remember.

Be friendly. We are a small, close knit community. We tend to clump and clique. Be the person that greets the new kids. Introduce them around. You will have a lifetime fan and maybe a new friend. Given that our world is based on relationships, be the matchmaker. I still remember the people that were kind to me when I first got out of school. They will always be on my favorite list. Be on someone's favorite list.

<u>Be cheerful.</u> This one goes back to having a good attitude. Smile. Even on the 16 hour load-ins and during Tech Week. A little cheerfulness is better than coffee.

<u>Be dependable.</u> If you accept a gig, do not throw it over for a gig that comes along later. It does not matter if gig two is the most amazing gig ever. When you ditch people they remember and it will come back to bite you in the tush. Be dependable. If you say you will do something, do it. No excuses.

<u>Respect the position of others</u>. Let's face it. There will at some point in your life come a time when you are working for a jerk. That jerk will be an idiot and a pain in the tookus

and will make your life hellish. Sometimes you aren't being respectful of the person, you are being respectful of the position. The stage manager might be crazy, but they are still in charge and you need to respect their position. It doesn't matter if your boss is a whackadoodle. As long as they are your boss you need to respect their position of authority. Don't badmouth them. Don't try to undermine them. You either stay in the job or you move on. But you need to respect the work of others.

This is true even when the person isn't your boss. I once worked with a ballet. We were staging a new piece with new scenery and brand new costumes. The costume department had worked long and hard on these gorgeous, exquisite costumes. They had been up until all hours trying to get things finished and literally had made their fingers bleed sewing on sparkly things. At one point in rehearsal they brought a stunning white jacket up for one of the lead male dancers to try on to check for fit. When it didn't fit exactly the way he thought it should, he snatched it off and threw it across the stage. Threw it across the nasty, dirty floor. His temper tantrum could have ruined this magnificent work of art that they had been slaving over. These sweet ladies only wanted to make him look great onstage and he responded by being disrespectful and hateful. Fifteen years later that is all that I remember about the jerk. I still hope they stuck straight pins in his tights.

<u>No whining!</u> Okay, so the Boy Scouts don't have this one in their creed, but they should. It pretty much should be tattooed on everyone's head. No whining. Ever. You are not age three. Suck it up and move on.

<u>There ARE stupid questions.</u> I know you have been told your whole entire life that there is no such thing as a stupid question, but that is a lie. There are indeed stupid questions. If that question has already been asked 19 times it is a stupid question to ask again. Pay attention the first time. Clearly you are somewhat intelligent if you have managed to make it this

far in life. Pay attention to what the crew chief/director/stage manager is telling you. Write it down if your memory stinks. Don't be the airhead that keeps asking the same thing. You will make people crazy and they will hate working with you.

The exception to this rule is if you are asked to do something tricky/hard/somewhat dangerous like running a table saw or tying in power or, I don't know, arc welding perhaps and you aren't completely confident in your abilities. In that case, ASK THE QUESTIONS! It isn't worth getting hurt over. Do pay attention though so that next time you are asked to saw/weld/deal with power you will know what you are doing and won't die a horrible, mangled death.

Chapter Three- Time Management

"Don't say you don't have enough time. You have exactly the same number of hours per day that were given to Helen Keller, Pasteur, Michelangelo, Mother Teresa, Leonardo da Vinci, Thomas Jefferson, and Albert Einstein."
H. Jackson Brown[5]

Theatre people are not, as a general rule, morning people. Many of us have trouble with time. There are those that say it is because we tend to be super creative, right brained based and fairly non-linear. Perhaps. It doesn't really matter what we are because, sadly, the world is time oriented and very linear. Morning people rule the world and we are left to cope.

What do you do? Start with prioritizing your activities. Make a list and then mark things

---

[5]

http://quotations.about.com/cs/inspirationquotes/a/Time10.htm

down in order of importance. Sometimes we tend to do the thing that catches our attention first instead of what is most urgent. Figure out what is most important throughout the day and get that done first.

Understand what you can realistically achieve with the time available. We almost never estimate time correctly. We like to think that we have all the time in the world to get things done, but that isn't true. You will have to learn to realistically budget your time so that you do not overbook or double book. Boss B does not care that Boss A kept you late. They only care that you have screwed their world. If you are constantly late or are blowing them off they will not want to hire you again.

Know that meetings will always take longer than you think. A one hour meeting never takes just one hour. A six hour call often runs long. Nothing ever takes the amount of time you think it will take. Plan accordingly. Make sure to leave open blocks of time between activities to allow for overflow and travel (contingency time). Murphy's Law dictates that if you are running late there will be a massive pileup on the interstate. If you are early, your drive will be clear sailing. For the sake of mankind, be early to keep the interstates clear for the rest of us. And always wear your seatbelt.

<u>Take a break</u>. While the urge is there to take all the work available, you still must schedule time to care for yourself. Once you start freelancing it is terribly tempting to agree to all of the work you can get. There is an urgency to fill your calendar, because there are times when the phone doesn't ring and there is no money coming in. Make sure during the times of plenty that you allow time for your body to recharge. Back to back 80 hour weeks will suck the life out of you. There was a point in my freelancing past that I made the decision to take at least one day a week off. That was the day I did laundry and bought groceries and cleaned the house. (HA!

Actually, that was the day that I napped all day to catch up on sleep and then frantically did laundry that evening. You can buy groceries pretty much 24/7 so you can totally do that chore on the way home from a gig when you are awake anyway.)

I know I have said this before, but do not blow off one gig for another. It will come back to haunt you. We really, truly do talk to each other so we know who is and who is not dependable. Blowing off a gig is the worst thing you can possibly do.

Helpful Time Management Hints:

Use To Do lists! Trust me. As you age you will forget things from one minute to the next, especially if you are sleep deprived. Get into the habit of writing stuff down. There are a gazillion phone apps that do this very thing. Get one and get in the habit of using it.

Use a calendar/day planner and check it before taking on new commitments. I am a huge personal fan of Google Calendar. It is free. It transfers between phones and computers. You can do multiple, color coded calendars that show up at the same time so you can see at a glance what is coming up.

How to Use a Calendar:

- Start your calendar by filling in all the non-negotiable dates for the year (family obligations, etc).

- Next fill in High Priority commitments, leaving a contingency window around them (things like work calls, auditions, rehearsals, shows).

- Lastly fill in regular maintenance commitments (doctor appointments, laundry, groceries, car maintenance, etc).

- The holes left over are free time.

Use your calendar to keep track of mileage, money spent, etc. (anything deductible). You need to save receipts and all that, but it is also a GREAT idea to keep track of this stuff directly on your calendar. If you do it as a separate thing on your Google calendar your tax guy will love you. Trust me. You will not remember this stuff in March/April when you finally sit down to get your taxes done. You are already going to have to write down gig appointments in your calendar. You might as well write down expenses in the same place.

Use short term daily planning. Well, duh. You need to know what you are doing from day to day. Write it on that calendar so you don't forget.

Use long term yearly planning. You will potentially book out gigs months in advance. You need to be able to see the big picture a year at a time.

Know that overbooking only leads to stress and a job poorly done.

Make the schedule and stick with it!!!!

Revisit past weeks and revise upcoming events to show a more realistic plan. If a company consistently goes past your scheduled call time make a note that they will be letting you go late in future calls.

Chapter Four: Punctuality

*"Tardiness often robs us of Opportunity."
Machiavelli*[6]

Punctuality is a huge component of time management. I will confess that I am horrible about time. I don't feel the passing of time like other people apparently do. This is a great job skill when I am working on a design or cueing or painting. It is horrible when I am trying to get ready in the mornings or be somewhere at a particular time. To that end I have had to learn some coping skills in an effort to look like a responsible adult.

Coping Skill #1:

<u>Buy an alarm clock</u>. Or three. Your cell phone alarm clock will not drag you out of bed when you are sleep deprived or at some hideous time of morning. As a freelancer it is <u>unlikely that you will work</u> consistent hours.

---

[6] http://www.brainyquote.com/quotes/quotes/n/niccolomac383742.html

Your body clock is going to be all screwed up. Get a really good (translate: loud and obnoxious) alarm clock. Have one that plugs into the wall and at least one (other than your cell phone) that uses batteries. They make alarm clocks now that roll off your bedside table so you have to get up and catch them to turn them off. I've seen some that turn lights on. Most will play music. I've even seen one that makes you complete a math problem before the alarm will quit. Do what you have to do to get yourself out of bed. I have three. There is one by the bed, one in a dock near the bed and one in the bathroom so I have to physically get up to turn it off. One way or another I am getting up.

Your other alarm clock option is to get a dog. Seriously. There is no turning that baby off. When my dogs (who are used to waking up at 6:30am) decide that the day has started, we get up. On the rare day that my befuddled, sleepy brain thinks it can just ignore the dogs and they will give up, I end up with a cold nose shoved in my face from Dog A and an intent stare from Backup Dog. It is easier to just get up and let them go out.

(Cats work too, but aren't as dependable unless you traditionally feed them something yummy first thing. I have found though that the cat is just as likely to wake you up super early in an effort to get the treat they want when they want it. Or perhaps they will ignore the treat completely. Cats don't seem to care if you are late.)

Coping Skill #2

Coffee... mmmmmm.... If you have spent any time at all in theatre it is highly likely that you have learned to drink coffee (probably along with some other highly questionable habits that we won't go into but that you should probably stop doing because they are really bad for you). Get yourself one of those snazzy auto-program coffee pots. It will turn itself on at the appropriate time and the smell of Coffee Nectar will drag you out of bed and make your eyes sproing open. Good times.

**Disclaimer- I personally have never learned to drink coffee. I am always bitterly disappointed that it doesn't taste like it smells. So this one won't work for me and the other non-coffee drinkers. The dog may be your only option.

Coping Skill #3

<u>Do as much as you can the night before your gig.</u> Your mom was right when she told you to lay out your clothes the night before. Go ahead and pack your gig bag and have it by the door. Know what clothes you are wearing and make sure they are ready to go. Pack your lunch/beverages. Make sure your tools are where they need to be. Go ahead and take the trash out. Whatever needs doing that can be done BEFORE you go to bed, go ahead and do it. You will be happier the next morning.

Coping Skill #4

<u>Allow yourself a window of emergency time.</u> Something stupid will happen if you don't. This is the whole premise behind Murphy's Law. Pad your morning with enough time to allow for minor transportation issues, clothing malfunctions, food trauma, tool breakage and coffee spillage. When you have only allowed enough time to do what HAS to be done you are tempting disaster. Your crew chief will not care why you are late. He will only care that you are late. Don't be.

Section Two- Finding a Job

"If you call failures experiments, you can put them in your resume and claim them as achievements." Mason Cooley[7]

Chapter Five: Marketing Yourself

Resumes

By now you should know what a resume is. You probably already have one (hopefully!). If not, you need to get started. A resume is how you sell yourself to a prospective employer. A quick Google search will show you many, many styles of resumes and templates for making one. They actually aren't all that difficult to make, which is good, because you will need multiple resumes tailored to a variety of jobs. Keep a running resume list with everything you do on it.

---

[7] http://www.brainyquote.com/quotes/quotes/m/masoncoole394820.html

Draw from this to build your final resume. DO NOT falsify information on your resume! I repeat, we are a very tiny world and we talk to each other. If you lie or even fudge just a little on your resume you will eventually be found out. Don't do it. If your resume is lame then you need to look at the work you are doing and do better work.

Things I Look For in a Resume:

- Neatness and spelling count. There is a reason for the existence of spellcheck. Use it.

- Make your resume visually appealing. This does not mean use fancy, schmancy paper or weird fonts or distracting graphics. This means when I look at your resume it should be logical and orderly and appealing. We are a visual craft. Show me that you have those skills.

- Keep the font at 10pt or larger. Most of the people doing the hiring are old with tired eyes. If I have to fight to read your resume I will give up and move on to the next person.

- Keep a resume to one page only. Learn to sum up. This should be fairly simple since you are tailoring your resume to the job for which you are applying.

- Keep it simple. Use a high quality plain paper. Do not use paper with patterns or overwhelming textures. Do not use elaborate fonts. Times New Roman is your friend. Broadway is not, nor are any of the script fonts.

- Include a current address that is not necessarily your school address. School mail sometimes shuts down during the summer. You need an address where mail will actually get to you in a timely fashion. Your parents' address is okay. Trust me. Your folks will help you in pretty much any way they can to ensure that you are gainfully employed.

- Check your email address. Please, please, PPUHHHLEEEZE do not include a stupid email address like suksbeer69@gmail.com or blondegurltech@aol.com or anything else stupid and juvenile and cutesy. You can get all sorts of email accounts for free these days. With Gmail alone you can get multiple addresses. Go NOW and make up a real, honest to gosh, grown up email address and start using it. Try for FirstnameLastname@gmail.com or something similar. You might have to get clever if you have a fairly common name. Make it something that won't embarrass your mother if a prospective employer read it out loud to her. You're a big kid now. Make sure your email address reflects that.

- Along those same lines, check your cell phone and make sure that your voice mail sounds professional and mature. If it uses hold music make sure that it is professional and not highly annoying. I have hung up on more than one voice mail that blasted obnoxiously loud music at me. Keep it professional.

CV (curriculum vitae)

A curriculum vitae is used for academic positions (and medical jobs, but let's face it, you have a theatre degree so that likely won't come up). It is loosely translated as "course of life" and is an overview of your life and skills. A CV is more complete than a resume and can be two or more pages long. There are multiple websites and multiple templates available for a CV, so do a little Google searching and see what pops up. You can also explore online CV services like VisualCV.com. The joy of something like that is that you can link to it on a business card and don't have to haul around a lot of paperwork with you.

Business cards

You need some. They are relatively inexpensive and very portable. This is where you can show off your creativity. As long as your name and contact info is prominently displayed, the card itself can reflect your skills and abilities. There are many, many places online that offer nice cards at a low price. My personal favorite at the moment is moo.com and not only because the website sounds like a cow. They have an option that allows you to upload up to 50 photos to put on the back of the cards. In our visual world this is ideal. My current business cards have my favorite design moments from the last several shows that I have done. People are now collecting them like playing cards. "Hey, I don't have a *Hamlet* yet. Let me have one of those." It allows me to show off the quality of my work and helps to keep me on the forefront of their mind. Isn't that the whole point of marketing? Whatever you end up with, make sure that your grown up email address and a usable mailing address are on there. If you have a website or online CV put that on there as well. You want to be easily accessible. Keep a stack of these in your wallet or in your purse and learn to pass them out like candy.

Website/blog

If you are in a visual field you need to have some sort of visual representation online. It doesn't matter if you do design or tech or performance. You need a place online to showcase what you do. The good news is that there are any number of places where you can do this for free. I like www.blogger.com, but I am pretty Google driven. A quick internet search turned up all sorts of options. Pick your favorite and go to it. Make sure that the photos you are using are clear and of the highest quality. If you are doing shows for school they likely hire a professional photographer to come in and make archival photos for your program. See if you can get copies of those photos. If no professional shots are available, you need to learn to make quality photographs of your work or make friends with someone who can do that for you. Photographs and video are the evidence that you can do what you claim. You can also scan technical drawings and put those on your site. Make sure your webpage shows your skills. A picture truly is worth a thousand words.

Portfolio

A portfolio is a visual tool that shows your skills and range of abilities, as well as your ability to communicate complex ideas clearly and succinctly. Pick a format that best highlights your skills and is appropriate to your target audience. Make sure that you use only your best work. Do not include work from high school. The more professional or semi-professional work you can include the better. Over time make sure that you go back through your portfolio and shuffle out the older, less adept work and add in newer, better work. Make sure to use quality photographs and be neat.

There are several ways to make a portfolio. A Scrapbook style is made by physically cutting and pasting photographs into a blank scrapbook. This is time consuming and can get messy, but it does allow you to easily change out work over time if you pick a binder type scrapbook. Option B is a photo book. Places like Shutterfly and Snapfish allow you to import photos to the site and arrange them in a template. They will then print your project out as a real book. The downside is that you cannot add or delete photos after the project is printed. The good news is that it looks very professional.

A sample kit is a portfolio with physical examples of your work. If you do technical drawings or renderings or scenic art work this is where you want to present this work. Make sure that the physical carrying case for your work is of the highest quality that you can afford. Don't go crazy, but presentation is everything. Make sure that it is big enough to hold your projects, but not so big that it is a hassle to store or carry around. You can find portfolios at art stores and online at places like Amazon.com.

Chapter Six: Networking

"It isn't just what you know, and it isn't just who you know. It's actually who you know, who knows you, and what you do for a living."
Bob Burq[8]

Our industry is all about who you know and who knows you. We are such a tiny world in the grand scheme of things that most jobs come about because of contacts. It is imperative that you start networking early on in order to make those contacts. There are a host of conferences for college students. Take advantage of these opportunities while they are around. You should go to as many workshops and meet-and-greets as possible while you are there. Branch out from your immediate school group and meet people from other places. Be charming. Be chatty. Make friends. Those are the people that you will work with later on down the road. We tend to hire our friends for gigs. You need to be out there networking.

---

[8] http://theentrepreneurmind.com/?p=1635

Conferences to try:

KCACTF (Kennedy Center American College Theatre Festival)- This one tends to be more for actors and playwrights, although they do have a nice design competition. It showcases plays by different colleges and gives feedback.

SETC (Southeastern Theatre Conference)/NETC (Northeastern Theatre Conference)/etc. **There are versions of this for every part of the county** See if your college is taking a group and go. It is more fun than you can imagine and you will meet tons of people. If your college does not participate, start a campaign to attend or just get a group together and go. This one is pretty evenly mixed for actors and technicians. There are a ton of workshops covering a full range of subjects. One of the main highlights is the job fair. Auditions for summer stock and grad schools are held, as well as design competitions. There are several meet-and-greets along the way as well. I know SETC members have access to an online job search forum. I believe some of the other groups do the same.

USITT (United States Institute for Theatre Technology)- This one is for techs only. There are some workshops and a lot of exhibit floor showcases. There are usually a lot of really interesting technical "toys" to play with and the vendors are good to answer questions about their products. It is a great way to see what all is out there.

LDI/PLASA- LDI is the biggest technical theatre trade show in the country. It is currently alternating between Las Vegas and Orlando, although there are rumors that it might be moving to a third venue. While there are some workshops and classes, the big draw of LDI is that it is when all of the new equipment is released to the public. If a vendor has some snazzy new toy they will begin marketing soon, it is pretty much guaranteed to make it to LDI. This is the best place to see new stuff. Plus, it is like trick-or-treating for techies. Most booths offer some sort of swag, so you can come away with a goodie bag of nifty things. It is all techies all the time, so be prepared to wear a lot of black and be casually aloof.

PLASA is a smaller version of LDI held regionally. It will have a smaller exhibit floor and fewer workshops and classes, but it is usually free to attend and located closer to where most people live. PLASA is trying out the smaller format in select locations with the intent to spread these out across the country.

ArtSearch is an online site that matches job seekers with job openings. It is a subsidiary of Theatre Communications Group and requires a membership fee to join. It is a great way to hook up with jobs though. Some schools have a school membership that students are allowed to access. Ask before you spend your own money. If you are seriously searching though, this might be a good option for you.

Summer Stock is the best way to network. There is something about slaving away on a show together that cements the bonds of love.

There are summer stock theatres all across the country. Most will pay a pittance for the amount of work that you are doing. Some will actually ask you to pay them (Williamstown Theatre Festival comes to mind). At least once in your life you need to do a summer stock summer, if only so that years later you can relate how you slogged through the heat and snow uphill both ways to finish not one, but two (or possibly ten) shows simultaneously. You will get a lot of very practical experience and will meet all sorts of people from all across the country. And you will probably get the tshirt to prove it.

Graduate School is always a good option, but isn't 100% needed unless you want to eventually teach. You have to have at least a MFA to teach. I had a great time in graduate school and learned a ton. It is a swell way to meet people, but it is expensive. Most graduate programs are also now asking that you get a couple of years of real life experience before you come back to school. If you do decide to go to graduate school, do your homework to find the right one for you. Each program will have a slightly different emphasis and will be directing their graduates down a particular path. Decide where you want to end up before spending a lot of money starting down the road. Your perfect graduate school will pay you an assistantship to go to school so your costs are covered.

Internships can be good and bad. Some internships are nothing more than a cover for free slave labor for the organization. The intern learns nothing and spends all their time doing grunt work for free. A good internship will help you learn more about your craft or will enable you to work with someone supremely talented in your field. The goal is to make it a great experience for you, not necessarily for the organization. As a young designer/tech/performer a lot of people will ask you to work for free to "gain experience" and to "build your resume". While both are excellent things, you need to make sure that the work you are doing will actually do that. As a designer, I take work for a number of reasons. Sometimes I do it because of the project. It will satisfy me on an artistic level to get to work on that production. Sometimes I do it because of the people involved. I will either learn something or have a great time or both. Sometimes I do the work as a favor to help out a pal. We work in a "I'll scratch your back if you scratch mine" kind of world that runs on favors. If you can be helpful you should. Sometimes I take a job because the money is good or because I need the money. That's a pretty rotten reason if that is your only reason, but we can't function without funding, so it does come into play. An internship works the same way. You need to gain something artistically, emotionally, physically or financially from the endeavor. If it doesn't fulfill any of these things you need to keep looking for a better fit.

Chapter Seven: Interview Skills

"Genius- the ability to produce fantastic amounts of equally fantastic BS that all makes perfect sense." Jason Zebehazy[9]

Once you have submitted your amazing resume, hopefully the next step will be a face-to-face interview. This is an important moment. Some people look great on paper and stink in the interview. Others are just okay on paper but completely nail the interview portion. In a perfect world you will, of course, be brilliant in both.

At this point in your life, if you have not done so already, you need to develop the art of thinking on your feet. I used to teach my students that they needed to have an appropriate answer to any question that was thrown at them. As designers, "I don't know" was not an acceptable response. I'm not suggesting that you lie. I am suggesting that you think fast enough to have a plausible

---

[9] http://thinkexist.com/quotes/jason_zebehazy/

answer to questions. You will be better at this if you have done your research. Know the company to which you are applying. Research, research, research. It does not impress me when a prospective employee comes in and asks if we do sound. I work for a lighting company. We have never done sound. It isn't that hard to find that information out. Know the company before you come in to talk.

Practice talking in front of a mirror first if you are not comfortable talking to strangers. You can also video yourself with your handy dandy cell phone. Truthfully, at this point of your college career you should be able to talk to anybody without freaking out. You are, after all, theatre majors. If you aren't then you need to get out and practice more. Go to the conferences and chat up people at the exhibit booths. They will be glad to talk to you, you will potentially learn something about something new and you will be able to practice your talking skills.

Do a quick Google search for interview questions and read through the stack of articles listed. Think about those questions and come up with some answers. It is more likely that they won't ask you any of those particular questions, but the practice will get your brain moving.

Dress neatly. You can't go wrong with a nice pair of slacks and a decent collared shirt, no matter whether you are male or female. Men, go get a decent sports coat and tie. Ladies, you also can't go wrong with a nice skirt or dress. Unless your research tells you that this company is all about the eclectic, an interview is not the best time to wear your funky clothes. Clothes tell the interviewer who you are before you ever open your mouth. Be sure of what you are saying. Unfair or not, you will be judged. Choose wisely.

Wear something comfortable. This is probably not the time to break in a brand new pair of shoes or wear something you have never worn before. Make sure that you can move comfortably and that your clothing stays in place and stays neat. This is not the time for a wardrobe malfunction.

Limit the amount of perfume/cologne. I realize that you think it smells terrific. Not everyone will agree. In addition, there are those with allergies. Your cologne might send their sinuses raging for days. Don't bathe in the stuff. A little dab will do you. Or perhaps none at all!

Make sure that you are clean. I really shouldn't even have to say this, but take a bath, brush your teeth, have clean hair, and use deodorant (the real stuff, not the holistic crystal things that never work.). Make sure that your clothes are clean and ironed if need be. Look as nice as you can possibly look.

Smile! There is no crying in baseball or in interviews. Smile. Be positive. Let the interviewer see your fabulous personality. Be charming. Be the person that they remember at the end of the day.

Between your resume, portfolio and interview a prospective employer should be able to tell who you are. Make all three the strongest you possibly can and go for it!

Chapter Eight: Types of jobs

While non-theatre majors tend to get out and take what we would call "normal" jobs, you my theatre loving friend, likely will not. To that end, you need to know the types of jobs that are out there waiting for you.

A Full time employee is an employee that works 30-40 hours a week. The employer often pays taxes, health insurance and other benefits for the employee. The job has no identified end date. This is the Holy Grail of jobs. Lots of security, better financial situation, sunshine and unicorns everywhere. Sadly, there aren't that many of them in theatre unless you are willing to get a little creative in how you use your theatre degree. More on this later…

A Part time employee is an employee that works around 20-30 hours a week or less. The employer generally pays taxes for the employee, but no other benefits. The job has no identified end date. You have probably had a job like this before while in school or during the summers.

A Seasonal employee is an employee contracted to work from a specific starting date until a specific end date. Usually seasonal workers work the summer months or holiday seasons. The employer possibly pays taxes and sometimes pays other benefits as well. A lot of theatre jobs are seasonal.

A Freelance employee is an employee hired job to job. They are usually paid hourly. Sometimes taxes are paid by the employer, but no other benefits are paid. A lot of your tech jobs start as freelance work. Freelancing can be loads of fun, because you can pick and choose what jobs fit your schedule. It can also be terrifying, because there is no guaranteed amount of work or money. You will have to figure out your own health insurance and other benefits and that gets expensive.

An Independent contractor is a worker hired for a specific task. The employer does not take taxes out and provides a 1099 tax form instead of a W-2. No benefits are provided. This one can be tricky. It all comes down to control. If you provide your own tools and gear and set your own schedule you could be an independent contractor. If tools and gear are provided and you are given a schedule to follow then you are an employee, not an independent contractor. A lot of design gigs are considered independent contractor work. Be very careful about this one. As an independent contractor YOU are responsible for 100% of your tax load. If you don't plan for it April 15th will be a big shock. The government doesn't care that you spent the money already. They will want their cut and it can be around 25% or more of the total amount. You will have wanted to stash that away in a savings account so you can pay the tax bill.

Chapter Nine- Traditional and Non-traditional jobs

So you have this shiny new theatre degree and you are convinced that you will be on Broadway or working at a really swell regional theatre full time, living the good life with all your theatre pals. Good times. And I will be winning the lottery tomorrow and moving to Tahiti where my cleaning fairy and pool boy will cater to my every whim. Sunshine and unicorns everywhere! Life is good!

Okay, seriously. There are perhaps three jobs opening up on Broadway at any given moment and fewer than that at regional theatres. You and the other eleventy billion recent graduates are not likely to be on anyone's hiring radar unless you have wisely spent your undergrad years toning up a stellar resume and portfolio.

So what are you to do? You want to do something with that degree, right?

Traditional Jobs:

Traditional theatre jobs, while rare, do exist. If you have a Scene Design emphasis you will likely consider the following:

- Scenic Designer, Assistant Scenic Designer
- Technical Director, Assistant Technical Director
- Carpenter, welder, craftsman
- Propsmaster, props crew
- Stagehand
- Scenic Charge, Scenic Artist

As a Lighting Design student you will consider these jobs:

- Lighting Designer, Assistant Lighting Designer
- Master Electrician, Assistant Master Electrician
- Electrical crew, board op, follow spot op

Is the costume shop more your forte? Consider these options:

- Costume Designer, Assistant Costume Designer
- Shop Foreman, Assistant Shop Foreman
- Buyer, Draper, Cutter, Stitcher, Craftsperson
- Hair and Makeup Artist
- Dressers, run crew

Sound Design emphasis will look at:

- Sound Designer, Assistant Sound Designer
- Sound Engineer, sound crew

Stage Manager skills will net you these jobs in the traditional theatre world:

- Assistant Stage Manager
- Production Manager

An acting emphasis will garner you work as an actor and directing will, logically enough, get you work as a director or assistant director. Playwrights are pretty much on their own.

Non-traditional jobs:

There are any number of non-traditional jobs out there if you are willing to think outside the proscenium arch. You will have to think creatively and dig a little harder, but these non-traditional theatre jobs can be very fulfilling and pay as well, or better, than traditional jobs.

Roadhouse
A roadhouse is defined as a venue that does not produce its own shows, but rather receives touring productions. Most major cities will have at least one roadhouse if not more. Roadhouses hire technical directors, stagehands, lighting techs (and occasionally designers), followspot ops, sound engineers (and occasionally designers), front of house personnel and arts management types. They typically will have a few full time

jobs and a lot of freelance workers. To get a job at a roadhouse you would need to apply in person at the venue. Details will vary from venue to venue, so do a little research on your particular location. This is one of the venues where word of mouth is important. Talk to those people older and wiser who have worked there all ready to get the scoop on how they hire. If you don't know anyone already working there (and clearly that means you need to network more), call and ask for the Human Resources department and ask about their hiring policies.

Roadhouses are fun because there are usually a great variety of shows coming through. You get to experience everything from Broadway tours to the ballet to the opera. Working in a roadhouse is also an excellent way to network. I have known a number of people who met touring companies while working at a roadhouse and later they went out on the road with them.

Cruise ships
A quick check of Wikipedia tells us that there are roughly 1000 cruise ships circling

the planet at any given time from the 50 major cruise lines operating around the world.[10] According to the American Association of Port Authorities and the Florida-Caribbean Cruise Association, there are a total of 314,000 cruise ship jobs available (in all areas, not just theatre).[11] Cruise ships contain fully functional, working theatre spaces and sometimes more than one. The large cruise ships have theatre staffs equal to some large regional theatres.

The downside is that you can be away from home for months at a time. Your accommodations will not be fancy and you will likely be sharing space with a stranger. You will work hard without a ton of downtime. If there are huge technical problems you will need to be able to fix them yourself as sending the gear out for service will be hard to do. You will not be enjoying all the luxuries of the cruise. The good news is that the pay is pretty good. All of your needs are covered while

---

[10] http://en.wikipedia.org/wiki/List_of_cruise_lines

[11] http://www.statisticbrain.com/cruise-ship-industry-statistics/

onboard ship (no rent or utilities!). You get to see the world (on your downtime you can visit the islands you are cruising). It can be a great experience and be a lot of fun.

Be sure that this is the life for you before taking on a cruise. Tours run three months or longer. Once you start you are pretty much there.
To get a job on a cruise ship do an online search for the individual cruise lines or check with a turnkey (full service) company like Gary Musick Productions in Nashville, Tennessee. Cruise ships hire technical directors, production managers, stage managers, sound engineers, lighting techs, lighting board ops, followspot ops, stagehands, costume crew, makeup artists, actors, dancers and musicians. Usually the scenic, lighting and costume design are done before the ship leaves dock.

Casinos
Google Las Vegas and count the number of shows running right now. I almost put a number in this book, but it keeps changing so fast I can't keep up. These are full scale Broadway style shows, not to mention the plethora of comedy shows, tribute shows, magic shows, headliners and "adult" shows. Cirque du Soleil alone has eight major shows running just in Las Vegas.

Casinos are located primarily in Las Vegas and Atlantic City, but there are casinos located in at least 40 of the 50 states.[12] Most of the major casinos in Las Vegas produce shows inside their hotels. There are fewer shows in Atlantic City. Fewer still in the random casinos scattered across the country. Most of the entertainment in the non-Vegas casinos is limited to concerts and music acts. Riverboat casinos are generally JUST gambling. If there are entertainment venues on board they are almost always just musical acts.

Shows in Las Vegas run the gamut from magicians to comedy acts to musical revues

---

[12] http://www.americancasinoguide.com/casinos-by-state.html

to fully staged theatrical productions like Cirque du Soleil. The larger theatres in Vegas are fully functioning, high tech theatrical spaces. They hire all of the regular technical positions, as well as actors, dancers, musicians and stage managers.

How to get a casino job:
> Some casinos list their employment opportunities online. Do a search for the facility that interests you most and see what jobs are open.
> Some casinos have tables at hiring fairs (in our world that would be USITT, SETC, LDI and the like).
> Some jobs are word of mouth.
> Some jobs are by show (Cirque du Soleil). Apply directly to Cirque du Soleil.

Amusement and Theme Parks
According to the International Association of Amusement Parks and Attractions there are around 450 amusement parks in the United States.[13] Central Florida (Orlando)

---

[13] http://www.iaapa.org/resources/by-park-type/amusement-parks-and-attractions/industry-statistics

has the largest concentrations of theme parks, but almost every state has a theme park (Alaska doesn't have a theme park, but they do have a water park, oddly enough).[14]

Theme park shows can be HUGE productions. Parks like Disneyworld, Disneyland, Universal Orlando and Dollywood stage everything from simple musical acts to fully staged theatrical spectacles. Theme parks hire every single technical job as well as herds of actors, dancers and musicians.

How to get hired at a theme park-

>Most every theme park hires seasonal workers for these positions. Every now and then you run across a full time gig, but don't count on it. Most full time work goes to people that have done seasonal work already and are known by the administration. Most parks post their job openings online. Pick your favorite park and do a little online research to see what is available

---

[14]

http://themeparks.about.com/cs/usparks/l/blparksbystate.htm

Some parks attend hiring fairs (like SETC, USITT and LDI) and go directly to colleges.

Most parks will schedule audition days and job fairs early in the year to get their summer employees. Do not wait until the last minute to apply.

Concert Touring

Touring is a staple of the lighting and sound industries. The benefit of touring is that the pay is usually great, the equipment exciting and new and the work can be a lot of fun. The downside is that it is a lot of constant, hard work. You are away from home a lot, mostly on weekends and holidays. You will spend a lot of time crammed in a bus with a lot of other people or crammed into an airplane with a lot of other people. If you are a hermit, this isn't the job choice for you.

Tours are crewed through specific companies, not through the band. At the moment, tours primarily leave from Nashville, New York, LA and Chicago. The best way to get a touring gig is to hire on with a full service production company in one of those cities. You will likely work in the shop at first until they trust you not to be an idiot. Once you have proven yourself and proven that you have a decent personality you possibly will get a bottom rung position. Touring gigs are all about networking. Personality matters since you will be with the same people 24/7 for months. This one is all about who you know and what they know about you!! It also helps to be young and zippy. There is a point that touring becomes too hard on your body. Tour while you can and bank the money for later when your body gives out.

Be aware that gender equality in touring is not exactly equal. This has slowly gotten better over the years, but sadly it is still easier to get a touring gig if you are male. I have only anecdotal evidence for this, as most companies will tell you they are equal opportunity employers, but when it comes to filling a tour bus they tend to still pick all men. Ladies, if you want it fight for it. Just be aware that it potentially will be an uphill battle. The good news is that most, if not all, of the other jobs are gender neutral. It's something about packing a tour bus that just doesn't want to go co-ed.

Tours utilize Technical Directors, Road/Personnel Manager (deals with people such as travel arrangements, money), Production Manager (deals with equipment and crews), Stage Manager (runs the show), the Advance team (makes sure everything is in order before the trucks/buses show up), Sound (Sound engineers, designers, monitor engineers, crew), Lighting (designer, board op, crew), Backline crew (maintain the musical equipment) and the Merchandise manager (deals with the swag for sale to the audience).

The Other Fine Arts
The arts outside of theatre are often overlooked. Working for a symphony, dance company or opera can be a great full time job. Symphonies hire a number of technical positions. Even a moderately sized orchestra will have a production manager, stage manager, audio engineer, lighting director and production assistants. Sound is, of course, vitally important to orchestras so they tend to spend more money hiring these people. To get this job apply directly to the symphony or the symphony hall.

Opera companies often have in-house costume shops with full time employees.
Generally they have an in-house production manager/stage manager as well.
Sometimes they have an in-house lighting, scenic and sound designers, but more generally they hire these as freelance positions.

Dance companies often have in-house costumers and technical staff. They will generally have at least an in-house production manager or stage manager. Sometimes there is an in-house TD/propsmaster. Often the lighting design and scenic design are hired in as freelance or as independent contractors. Production of scenery and lighting is external unless it is a very large company. To get this job apply directly to the company itself. Often these jobs are based on who you know.

Event Planner
A party planner/designer is essentially a stage manager with an eye for design or is a very organized designer. A good party planner will decide on all of the visual elements at the party and then marshal the vendors to get everything in place on time and under budget. Parties can cost hundreds of thousands of dollars. Events

include weddings, fundraisers, bar and bat mitzvahs, quinceanera parties, corporate events, funerals, wedding and baby showers, and just all around generic parties. These events often utilize lighting, sound, scenic design (décor), bars and catering, video, fabric rentals, floral arrangements, invitations, party favors, and valet services. Venues can be tents of all shapes and sizes, hotel ballrooms, barns, factories, private homes, sports arenas, corporate facilities, state and federal buildings, caves, farmers' markets, garages, forests, rooftops and open fields. Pretty much any space is fair game (and yes, I have done parties in every single one of those venues at some point in my past).

A good party planner has excellent people skills, is extraordinarily organized and is very self-motivated. All components of party planning can be broken into separate jobs. There are vendors for everything these days and a great many companies are making a living just designing the lighting or just designing the sound, or the decor. Find your niche and excel. How do I get this job? Either go work for an existing event planning company or strike out bravely on your own.

Churches

There are at least 1200 mega churches in America (those with 2000 or more in attendance on Sunday morning). According to a 2011 study by the Hartford Institute for Religion Research, 54% of mega churches are non-denominational. They tend to have contemporary services. They tend to have multiple services throughout the week on multiple campuses. Around 32% of American mega churches are in the southeast. Another 18% are located in the great lakes area. Approximately 70% of participants are under the age of 50 with the average age range being in the 30s-40s. [15] These large churches almost always have complete media and theatrical systems.

Theatrical work in churches is one of the fastest growing job opportunities out there. The mega-churches are building fully functional spaces that often outclass local theatres. They are installing complete sound systems to rival rock bands and lighting rigs better than most theatres. While a lot of the

---

[15] http://www.hartfordinstitute.org/megachurch/megachurch-2011-summary-report.htm

tech work is done by volunteers out of the church body, there is generally a TD or head tech position that is full time on staff. To apply for these jobs you would check with the individual church. Most churches will require you to be a member of their congregation, but not all.

Private Tech Companies

Most major cities have private tech companies. Do a Google search for your city of choice and see what pops up. Some specialize in lighting, some in sound, and some in Audio Visual. Some do all of the above (also known as turnkey companies). With most companies you will start out as a freelance technician and work your way up the ladder. To get this job apply directly to the company. Have a prepared resume with references. Be ready to fill out an application on site. Many private companies do drug testing before hiring.

Production Companies

There are scenic production houses that design and build scenery for parties, weddings, corporate events, fundraisers, awards shows, galas, halftime shows at the Super Bowl and NBA Finals. Somebody has to design and build all that stuff you see on TV. In addition, there are expos for pretty much everything these days. Someone has to design the booths. A lot of these booths are fully wired for lighting, sound and video. They are essentially sets designed for a very specific purpose (to showcase a product). They have to be built, painted, wired and assembled. These companies tend to be clustered in the major cities and a quick Google search will turn up scads of them. These production houses use full design teams, technical directors, carpenters, scenic artists, and lighting techs. To get this job apply directly to the production company. Be ready to fill out an application on site and have samples of your work available. Most jobs will be freelance, but there will be opportunities for advancement to full time.

High end department stores
In the larger cities store window display is a super competitive design field. Somebody has to decorate the stores and store windows, right? While most stores hire the production of window décor out to production houses, the design work is often done in house. In the larger cities (NY and LA) there is fierce competition to create the most intriguing window display. Scenic designers and lighting designers are used, along with fashion merchandising designers. To get this job you will need to apply directly to the store. Go visit New York around the Christmas holidays and check out the amazing work being done. It's scenic design on steroids!

Product Sales
So all this stuff we use has to come from somewhere. There are sales jobs in all of the technical areas, as well as sales of scripts and whatnot. Most moderately sized city will have local companies selling equipment and expendables in all of the technical areas (sound, lights, AV, makeup, costumes). In addition, distributers have sales reps over regions pushing particular products. ETC,

Strand, Altman, Rosco, GAM and Apollo are all lighting suppliers that have people in place to talk to dealers and to see that their product gets specified. The same is true in most of the technical fields. These jobs are usually full time and can pay okay. Sometimes they are commission based and other times you receive a salary. It will just depend on the company. If there is a product that you love, check to see who is selling it locally and see if they are hiring. You might just be able to convince others to love that product too.

System installer
System installers and field techs are the people that go put new dimming, lighting, sound, and projection equipment into new or remodeled spaces. If you like futzing around with equipment this might be the ideal job for you. To get this job you have to go through a dealer. You will likely need to work for them for a while before you can go to training. System tech positions are only awarded after you complete training (often at your own expense). Contact the company directly for more information.

Other random jobs
- University faculty
- High School faculty
- Theatre consultant
- Art directors
- Museum design/ Science Centers
- Riggers- for lighting, sound, scenery, aerial acts
- Prosthetic work
- Makeup artists (music videos, upscale makeup stores, modeling agencies, spas and salons, theatres, Halloween stores, personal makeup artist for celebrities, work with cancer patients)
- Special effects shops
- Community Centers (with theatres)
- Libraries (with theatres)

Section Three- Money, Money, Money

"A budget tells us what we can afford, but it doesn't keep us from buying it." William Feather[16]

Chapter Ten: Budgeting

I am going to take a leap and guess that you are most likely not that great with money. We right brain creative types generally aren't. However, money makes the world go around so you are going to have to suck it up and figure out how to deal with it. While I know that your tendency is to skip this chapter, don't do it. It may be painful, but you need to hear this stuff.

Before you get out of school you need to think about short term budgeting. This is your day-

---

[16]

http://www.brainyquote.com/quotes/quotes/w/williamfea130795.html

to-day money needs. Budgeting is not fun. We all want to buy what we want when we want it. Unless you win the lottery or marry well (and the odds of either are pretty nonexistent), you will have to budget with what will be a limited income.

Step one is to find a budget template. There are a gazillion on the internet or you can make one up yourself with Excel.

Look! Here's one I whipped together that you can steal:

Short Term Budget

Income:	Week 1	Week 2	Week 3	Week 4	Total
Check 1					
Check 2					
Check 3					
Check 4					
Weekly Total:					Total

Out go:	Projected	Actual	Difference		
Rent/Mortgage					
Food					
Car loan					
Fuel					
Cell Phone					
Internet					
Ins/car					
Ins/Health					
Ins/Home					
Utilities					
School loan					
Clothes					
Misc supplies					
Entertain $					
IRA					
Savings					
Emergency $					
Et cetera					
Total					

Make adjustments as needed. Or really, Google "Budget Template" and pick one that makes you happy. Just use something.

You will need to realistically estimate your income as a freelancer. Some weeks you will make a bucket load of money because you are working 80 hours and half of that is overtime. Other weeks you will make nothing. Literally, no money will come in the door because some months have no work available. You have to plan for the dry season. That is what your savings account is for. If you do not have anything saved there will be months that you won't have money to pay bills. Your landlord will not care that you can't find work, so plan ahead.

Stick to your budget! I know the temptation is there to buy new toys and eat expensive foods when the money is good. That is fine if you have enough saved to hold you over (three months of total bills). Just don't waste money during the good months and be left with nothing during the lean months. Winter is coming, my friends.

Avoid credit card use. If you cannot pay the card off at the end of the month, don't charge whatever you are thinking of charging. Credit cards are great when you are purchasing things online. They are handy to have in case of a huge emergency. Do not get in the habit of carrying a balance though. Once you lose control of the credit card you are sunk. They are so hard to pay back when you are broke. This will be your biggest financial struggle if you let it get out of control. The credit card companies will be courting you soon if they aren't already. Keep in mind that they want to make money off of you. They are not non-profit organizations. They make bucket loads of money off of interest payments and fees. Be very, very careful about using a credit card.

Bonus Paragraph!

You most likely have college loans that will start coming due once you graduate. Hopefully you have been able to keep these to a minimum, but more likely you have a heavy debt load hanging over your head the minute you have your diploma in hand. You really, really, REALLY want to get those paid off quickly. Probably they will be set up to be paid over ten years' time. You want to get those paid off in two or three. Adulthood is screaming up on you now. It is easier to live frugally in the first years after college than it is in your thirties. At some point you will want to upgrade your housing situation, get married, and make babies. All of those things are really expensive. Do whatever you need to do with your lifestyle so that the bulk of your paycheck can go towards paying off those loans. You will feel so much better once that last payment has gone in.

Long term planning

Okay, so I know that you are probably still in your 20s and the thought of retirement is waaaayyyyyy out there. I hate to tell you this, but life tends to just swoosh right on by and your old age will be here before you know it. If you wait until you are in your 40s before planning for retirement you have waited too late. It is unlikely that you will have a pension plan in theatre and social security is iffy at best. It behooves you to go ahead and start planning.

Interest is a crazy mathematical thing. I won't bore you with details (because, quite frankly I have no real idea how it works other than by math magic), but a tiny bit of money invested/saved at age 25 grows to astonishing amounts, whereas a tiny bit of money invested at age 45 only grows a tiny amount.

If you put $500 in an IRA at age 25 it will turn into $10,862 if withdrawn at age 65 (that is with no additional contributions and at 8%

interest**). If you wait until age 70 to pull proceeds the total comes to around $15,960. This is $10,362 of FREE MONEY, people. For which you did not have to work. It just magically accumulated while you were off doing other things. Since you will likely get chunks of money for graduation, putting $500 into an IRA at age 25 isn't all that hard. Let's face it. You spend more than that on electronics and toys. Go ahead and invest in an IRA and start the ball rolling. Any bank on the planet can help you out, although if you are smart you will Google this and find the best rates.

**All of this math was done using an online Roth IRA calculator like this one found at http://www.bankrate.com/calculators/retirement/roth-ira-plan-calculator.aspx. I did not do the math in my head because it is magic. You do not have to understand this stuff for it to work.

More math for you:

$500 in an IRA at age 25 plus $10/month= $44, 436 at age 65**

$500 in an IRA at age 25 plus $20/month= $78,010 at age 65**

If you wait until age 40 to do the same = $3,424 at age 65**

Seriously, people. This one is a no brainer even for the math impaired like us. You will thank yourself one day if you go ahead and start planning for retirement now. This is the number one thing I wish someone had told me when I graduated.

If you want to be even more prepared, find yourself a good money person to help you invest. There are people that actually like doing this stuff and they are really good at it. I know! It's weird to me too, but there you have it. Find one and become friends by paying them money to do this work for you. It is worth it in the end for those of us that are money math impaired. Find a math geek and let them use their powers for your good. Ask around. Actually, ask the old people you are working with and see if they know of someone reputable. You will be very happy you did.

Chapter Eleven: Taxes

[on filing for tax returns] "This is too difficult for a mathematician. It takes a philosopher."
Albert Einstein[17]

"Normal" jobs give you a W2 sometime in January. It lists what they paid you and what they paid in taxes. You will get one of these for every non-independent contractor job you work. My best/worst year I had fourteen of these. My tax guy wasn't happy.

A 1099 is the tax form given to independent contractors. In theatre you will often be considered an independent contractor. That means that you function as both the employer and the employee. All of the taxes that an employer usually pays become your responsibility. Normally an employer pays half of your tax load and then deducts the other half from your paycheck.

---

[17] http://www.tax-saving-professionals.com/tax-quotes/

If you are self-employed, you pay 100% of the tax load. This means that you must hold money out of that paycheck to pay your taxes.

The best, and pretty much only, tax advice I have is to get a good accountant. Come spring, my tax guy is my most favorite person ever. He understands this stuff and actually seems to like it. I just show up with receipts and mileage (which I have written down in my handy dandy calendar already) and he does magical things to make me and the government happy. Using an online tax program will not be in your best interest if you have any 1099s. Those programs handle one W2 fairly well, but just can't figure out what to do with our world. Same thing goes with the little strip mall tax shops. You need to find a real tax accountant. Ask around at work and see who people recommend. You want someone that does a lot of entertainment taxes. Our world is weird. You want someone that understands how we work.

A good tax accountant will let you know what you can and cannot deduct. There are all sorts of rules on this one, but the short answer is that if you spent money on the job you can *possibly* deduct it. This includes tools, clothing, mileage, food bought while on the job and anything you spent money on for that job. You can potentially even deduct things like your cell phone and trade magazine. Ask your tax person and see what is allowed in your area. The rules sometimes change, so having an up-to-speed accountant is a must.

Save your receipts. One of those expanding files is a great way to get organized by month. Staple together every receipt for each job so things are tidy. You might also write on it the name of the gig. It really helps to put this stuff in your calendar too so you have all the totals in one place. I have known people that take a picture of each receipt with their phone so that they have backup. Do whatever it takes so that you can keep track of the info. You will be very happy the following April.

Section Four : The World of Theatre

Chapter Twelve: Unions, LORT and other assorted animals

Depending on where you live, unions may very well be a huge part of your professional life. There are lots of arguments for and against unions. There are both positives and negatives involved. In theatre you often will not have a choice as to whether you will join a union or not. Either way, you need to be aware of what you are dealing with.

Right to work

Some states are known as "Right to Work" states, meaning that they have passed legislation that makes it illegal for business owners to require union membership. Alabama is a right to work state as is Arizona, Arkansas, Florida, Georgia, Idaho, Indiana, Iowa, Kansas, Louisiana, Michigan,

Mississippi, Nebraska, Nevada, North Carolina, North Dakota, Oklahoma, South Carolina, South Dakota, Tennessee, Texas, Utah, Virginia and Wyoming.[18] See the Department of Labor's website for more information http://www.dol.gov/whd/state/righttowork.htm If you work in one of these states you do not have to be in a union to work a job. There might be union jobs available (for example, some touring shows may still be union gigs), but most of the local work will not require a union card.

In the other states a union affiliation might be required to work on stage. There are a number of unions that control what we do. All of them have websites. It would behoove you to do a little research on them if you are living in or moving to those states. The rules for each union are very specific, so read up.

Most of you will have heard of **Actor's Equity Association (also** known as simply

[18] http://www.dol.gov/whd/state/righttowork.htm

Equity). Actor's Equity is the labor union for live theatrical performance (as opposed to film and TV). It controls both actors and stage managers. Getting your Equity card can be a rite of passage for a performer and among other things can be an indicator of skill level and ability. Go to http://www.actorsequity.org/ for more information.

The American Guild of Variety Artists represents performers in variety entertainment such as circuses, Vegas acts, magic shows and theme parks. There is some overlap with Actor's Equity. See http://www.agvausa.com for more information.

The Screen Actors Guild, also known as SAG, is the labor union representing working actors in film, television, industrials, commercials, video games, music videos and other new media. Their website is www.sagaftra.org.

For the technical among us, **IATSE** (International Alliance of Theatrical Stage

Employees) is the theatre labor union that represents stage hands, technicians, artists and craftsmen. It also includes those that do technical work on movies and television. See http://iatse.net for more information.

The United Scenic Artists is the labor union for designers and design assistants for entertainment design. This includes scenic artists, scenic designers, costume designers, lighting designers, and sound designers. Their website can be found at http://www.usa829.org.

The Stage Directors and Choreographers Society is the labor union for directors and choreographers. Their website can be found at http://sdcweb.org.

The American Guild of Musical Artists represents opera, dance and concert musicians. More information is available at http://www.musicalartists.org.

The **League of Resident Theatres** (LORT) gets included in this section even though it is not a union. LORT is a professional organization of not-for-profit regional theatres. There are currently 74 LORT theatres across the country. Membership levels are based on weekly box office receipts. I throw this in because I had no idea what it was when I got out of grad school and I probably should have. http://www.lort.org/

Bonus Chapter 13- Discretion

Ladies, this chapter is primarily directed at you, although guys can take heed as well. Despite all of our talk about gender equality and non-gender specific workplaces, the truth is that men and women are still treated differently. It just happens. We have made strides in the whole "equal pay for equal work" field and that is great. There is still work to be done in the Perception arena.

Women in tech: you are going into a male dominated field. It becomes more and more balanced every year, but it is still a man's world out there. There is a direct correlation between how you behave and how you are treated. To quote my sister, "Be classy, not trashy." If you want to be treated seriously, you need to be professional. Cutesy, girly won't work here. I'm not saying you have to be butch or cuss like a sailor, but if you present yourself as a giggly, silly airhead that is how you will be treated. And as unfair as it is, what you wear also matters. If you wear revealing clothes, you will not be treated like an equal player. You will not be taken seriously. You need to wear clothes appropriate to the work. If what you wear leaves you in danger of a "wardrobe malfunction" then it is not appropriate to wear to work.

I believe I have mentioned before that theatre people talk. We talk a lot. Biggest group of gossips EVER. People are going to talk about you. Be very, very careful about your reputation. You want to be known for the work you have done, not the people you have done. While it is somewhat inevitable that you will date coworkers, give yourself a little time to learn about people and their reputation. You can and will get a reputation for who you hang out with. There is no need to rush into relationships before you have scoped out the field.

I knew a guy that was engaged and living with said fiancée. Fiancée had a job that required a lot of travel and she was gone on tour for weeks on end. Boy decided that he was lonely and started "hanging out" with a fresh-from-college girl behind fiancée's back. Fiancée found out fast because **everyone in the industry knew what was going on and they talked about it.** I'm telling you, our gossip network is faster than light. Instantly boy became a pariah, fresh-from-college girl became an idiot and everyone sided with the fiancée done wrong. Boy also got kicked out of the house and the relationship, but we all agreed that was for the better for fiancée. Over a decade later, those impressions still hold true. The girl has never been terribly successful in the microcosm that is our industry because of her foolish early mistake. Boy is still thought of with disdain. Fiancée married a different man and is pretty much the princess. You want to be the princess. Classy, not trashy ladies.

Epilogue:

Getting your first job is exciting, but it is only the beginning. The trick is to stay employed for the next 50 years. The pay will likely stink and the hours will be horrible, but it will be loads of fun. If it isn't, you probably should start looking for a different world in which to work. It is, however, entirely possible to use that Bachelor of Theatre Arts degree. Now make your parents proud and go get that job!

I have been (mostly) gainfully employed in theatre for the last 20 years. I have worked for a variety of companies in a variety of capabilities. It has been a strange, weird, oddly compelling career. My mother still can't really explain to her friends what I do, but she is vastly entertained by the stories I bring home. I have worked with generous, caring, insanely talented people. I have also worked with real jerks. Clearly they didn't read the chapter on character.

This book is the result of talking to and working with both the jerks and the delightful souls. Be the delightful soul. Now go get a job!

Anne L. Willingham is the Educational Outreach Director at Bradfield Stage Lighting in Nashville, Tennessee. She received a Bachelor of Interior Design from the School of Architecture at Auburn University and a Master of Fine Arts from the University of Alabama in set and lighting design. After an internship year at the Alabama Shakespeare Festival, Anne moved to Nashville and joined the local theatre workforce serving as set and lighting designer for such groups as Vanderbilt Opera Theater, Montgomery Bell Academy, Shelter Repertory Dance Theatre, Nashville Children's Theatre, Mockingbird Theatre, People's Branch Theatre, Circle Players, and A.C.T. I. In addition to working professionally, Anne has served as an adjunct instructor for Belmont University and as the Assistant Professor of Lighting Design at MTSU.

Made in the USA
Middletown, DE
04 January 2019